the PROS *of* PROCESS

JAMES HALL

The Pros of Process
ISBN 978-099761-245-5
Copyright © 2016 James Hall
Tulsa, Oklahoma

the PROS *of* PROCESS

'Process' is a word that is very familiar to us today. We may know and understand what the definition of the word is, but do we really have a true understanding? So many times it is viewed in a negative way, but truly it can be a positive in our lives. We must see 'process' as a positive position in our lives, and through this book we are going to bring to light the pros and cons of 'process.' We are primarily going to uncover myths of the 'process' and give you a better understanding. We will focus on the "Pros of Process."

The Definition of Process:

"A series of actions or steps taken in order to achieve a particular end." Meanings of the same word are procedure, operation, action, activity, business, job, task—all these are the noun definitions of the word.

The verb definition of the word is "to perform a series of mechanical or chemical operations on something in order to change or preserve it. A continuous action or a series of changes taking place in a definite manner."

Contents

Chapter 1

INTRODUCTION TO THE PROCESS

There are many processes in life. **All living organisms depend on one another,** including humans. The one that we are most familiar with is that we were born as a baby, then we became a toddler, child, adolescent, teenager, young adult, adult, then senior adults. It was a process of natural time and natural growth to develop where we are today in our physical bodies. All living organisms depend on one another. If something is alive and living, then it took a process to get to the stage it is in or it takes continually being in a state of process to maintain its current state of being. This definition tells us that we are always in a process. If we are alive and breathing then we are in some type of process and it is natural, so we must look at it in a positive way of living and not a negative way.

Everything that has ever been made or invented was created through a process of following the right steps in order to get the desired results. Like baking a cake, you must use the right ingredients in the right amount in the right order to achieve the best results. If you use too much of a certain ingredient or do not follow the steps in order, your cake will turn out awful!

Process is a way of life we can't avoid like the desire to have a child. First, you can't have a baby by yourself—you must depend on someone else for this to take place. Remember my opening statement in this chapter? We must understand the importance of process and how important it is to follow the right steps to get the right results.

All the great inventors understood this and followed a process. If their outcome wasn't what they desired, they would go back and look at what they put in the process and what order they did it in to find their mistakes. Let's look at Thomas Edison. He said "Genius is one percent inspiration, ninety-nine percent perspiration." What he was saying is that it takes hard work to have something great. He invented the phonograph and the electric light bulb, and he was the first inventor to apply the principles of mass production and large scale teamwork to the process of invention. Edison has 1,093 US patents in his name, as well as many patents in the United Kingdom, France and Germany. He also invented the DC (direct current) power delivery system.

He received a lot of competition from companies installing AC (alternating current) systems. The AC systems the 1880's were used to light up large spaces like streets and businesses.

In 1885-1886, Westinghouse Electric saw fit to transmit AC over long distances and use thinner and cheaper wire than Edison's DC wire and allowed electric to not only be what lit up street lamps but also what was channeled for domestic residential use. Edison was losing lots of business and was about to lose everything, so he went back and reviewed the process by which DC worked and realized that his way was a better way than AC. He began to study the process of AC and realized it had many flaws in it and sent out a report telling people if they had AC power in their homes to be very careful because it was very dangerous. In a short amount of time, people started getting shocked and even killed in their own homes because of the AC power and everyone started using Edison's DC power. Westinghouse was on the verge of going under. Edison knew his low voltage DC was better; he had tested the process over and over and knew it was the best. When times got tough for him, he understood the power of process and wasn't moved by what he saw. All processes must contain certain elements to be a successful and proven process in order for the proper functioning of the organisms.

Chapter 2

THE STORY

I have become very familiar with the word 'process' over the last 10 years, both in my profession and also in my personal life. In order for my business to grow, I had to grow and I had to change my thinking. My perception of business and people had to change drastically, and my view of God had to change as well. I had to go through the process of change personally so I would flourish in life and become all God wanted me to be so that my business would flourish as well. Let me explain.

Many businesses fail simply because the owner does not want to change. People think they can stay the same and their business will flourish, and that is simply not true. In order for your business, church, or ministry to grow and to have success you must grow personally, you must take on a different mindset and transition the way you think. You must take on an ownership mentality to realize that the growth of the organization depends on how you perform. It is truly a mental transition of the process. In my profession, we are a production based company. In other words, we get paid a set rate no matter how long the job takes. So the faster we can get it started and finished, the sooner we can move on to the next job and the more money we make. All of our processes are the same. We fabricate and install granite countertops, so material changes constantly but the process stays the same. In other words, we cut the slabs the same, we polish the edges the same, we cut the sinks the same and we install the pieces the same way for every single job. Every single day that process doesn't change, and the process in which we do things has been created by how many times I've failed. I failed many times, but I kept on tweaking the process until it became right. And because the process does not change, our workers get very skilled in their jobs by doing the same work every single day. If they skip some steps in the process it shows up in the quality of the final product, and it will be a much lesser quality job.

As workers understand following the steps in the process of work, so therefore we must understand the process of our spiritual life in the same way. It takes time and effort doing the right things day after day and not taking short cuts. The process of our personal life works the same way as well. To illustrate further,

I'm going to share with you a time in my life where things weren't going very well.

The last thing I remember was just trying to get to the altar at the church. My life was such a mess. My family was devastated and my wife was crushed, so I knew I had to change my life but did not know how. All I heard the minister say was, "If you want to start the process of a new life, please come to the altar," so I practically ran to the front of the church because what he said sounded so good and I thought to myself, *"Yes, this is what I need."* The man leading the men's meeting began to pray for me. I closed my eyes so I wouldn't be distracted, and after about 20 minutes of him praying for me, my face was a mess. I had snot running everywhere but I did not care. Mentally I felt different, and physically I felt different, but when I went back to my seat only after a few minutes some of the same thoughts I had before I went to the altar began to take over my mind. I was very frustrated because I wanted to be changed, I wanted a better life, and the minister said, "Some things in your life are a process, and a process of change does not happen overnight." I really didn't know what to think. When I walked in the door that night, I looked at my wife and said, "I want my life back!" Tears were streaming down my face. I was ready for change.

The next morning I felt different. I had no more

desire for drugs or alcohol, but the desire to be involved in porn was overwhelming. I gave into it, and I continued to give into it. I cried and cried and yelled at God and said, "Why?" All I knew to do was to pray, so I began to pray. I told God to take this away from me, and in my heart I heard this voice say, "How can I take something away from you that I didn't give to you?" This blew my mind, so I stopped praying and I was like, "What??" I was very frustrated with it all.

Later that day, the minister from the men's meeting called me and ask me if he could help me get my life back on track. I said, "Yes, my life is a wreck!" He said, "I know, but I can help you," so I told him where I was in life and everything I was dealing with. I was very open and transparent at this point. I was sick of hiding everything from everybody; I was ready for change, ready for a new life! Thus began the process of him mentoring me on a daily basis, and I started the process of changing my life, which started with the way I was thinking. I will get back to this story a little later in the book.

Chapter 3

BUILT TO LAST

We are living in a microwave society where everyday people want things "right now" and people don't want to go through the process of what it takes to become great or have a great life.

Everyone wants the crown, but you have to go through the cross to get the crown. Everyone wants it right now, and we see it in what we eat. Fast food is one of the nation's largest killers, where processed foods are dominant in our society. These foods have been altered from their natural state, either for safety reasons or because it makes them easier to store or easier to use. It's not the processing that makes the food bad, it's what they put in it. So in food processing, the process they use is an excellent process, but the ingredients that they use makes processed food harmful to us. There are pros to the process—in other words, the process is good and there are positives in every process. While we are in the process, we must add the positive things to it in order to get the desired results. People view what they are going through in a negative way, but I'm here to tell you that whatever you're going through is for the positive, it is to make you better not bitter, stronger not weaker. We must put in the work and do the right things while we are going through the process of change and becoming what God wants us to be. Every person has to change, and no one has it all together. We all have things in our lives that are not right, either because of how we were raised or due to the influences in our lives from our formative years that have caused us not to think right or even act right.

Aristotle taught that we become who we are and what we are in life according to our gene pool—that we are what we are and do what we do because it is in our DNA, our genetic make-up. In other words, if a person is a doctor then his or her offspring will be a doctor, or if a person was a serial killer then his or her offspring would be a serial killer as well. Aristotle taught this to many followers until John Locke challenged Aristotle's teachings, arguing that we become what we are because of the environment that we grew up in as a child. Locke taught the theory of Tabula Rasa, which in Latin means "blank slate." He believed that every baby was born with a Tabula Rasa that at birth a baby's mind is completely empty (or a blank slate) that does not know anything about his or her parents. Locke taught that a baby from birth has the chance to become anything he or she wants to be in life as long as the environment that he or she is raised in is conducive to what he or she wants to be as an adult. This topic is the most debated topic in psychology today. The LGBT community is trying to get this theory taken out of psychology books because it proves that our genetic make-up has nothing to do with being a homosexual, thus meaning that they cannot blame it on the belief that states, "It's just the way I was born." This view completely destroys this type of thinking, and it proves that they do what they do because of choice.

So we have a lot of work to do to overcome how we were raised. Are you built to last? Do you have what it takes to overcome a bad mindset? It starts with receiving and accepting the blood of Jesus and what he did on the cross for you and I, causing us to realize that we need to change. If you look at others around you and say, "They need to change," the reason is the very faults that you find in others are the very faults that are actually inside of you. The reason you see it in someone else and it causes you to point the finger is the proof you and I need to change. Let me ask you again, are you built to last? It takes a real man or woman to admit their faults and their bad mindset that they have toward God, the church, Christians, business, marriage, or anything else in their life. Maybe you feel bitter or mad because of the environment you were raised in. If so, there is hope for you! Just keep reading this book and let the Holy Spirit start working on you right now. I believe there is hope for you. We must do our part and God will do his.

Chapter 4

IT IS THE WORK OF GOD

The process is a very positive thing in your life, because it is the working of God in your life and you must see the pros that are there and not focus on the cons. Let's look at all the positives that are beginning to take place and let's not focus on the negative things, because what we focus on the longest in our lives become the strongest in our lives. If you focus on the negative all the time the outcome will always be negative, so focus on the positive. There is light at the end of the tunnel, so just keep focused on God and the pros of what is going on, stay in prayer, stay in the Word, stay close to the Holy Spirit, and you must speak positive words and always speak life. Pray that all ungodly mindsets are broken in your life. Words are so powerful; they are creative, in his power God spoke and it was. The Bible says we were made in His image and His likeness (Genesis 1:26). The book of Proverbs are full of the power of our words (Proverbs 18:21, 6:2,). Jesus said it and it was so, and if we call ourselves Christians that means we are to be Christ-like. So, if we are to be like Christ then we should speak words of life! Our words are very powerful! God is trying to mold you and I to shape us into something strong and great!!! He is a good God and a loving Father and wants us to soar like eagles so that we can live the abundant life in Him. The position you see yourself in is the position that you pray and speak from, so if you see yourself as defeated or always the underdog or even the mistreated one, you will always pray and speak from a defeated position and you will have already disqualified yourself. That is what I did in my life for many years, but when I learned to view myself differently and saw myself the way God sees me, I began to understand what Ephesians chapter 2 tells us regarding how we have been raised and that we are seated with Him in heaven. I started seeing myself as the head and not the tail, above and not beneath.

Situations in my life started changing because my position changed in Him, which caused my thoughts and my prayers to change. You must see whatever process you're in is a good thing and embrace all the pros in it because if you do not you will go through the same process over and over again until you get it right. Some people never learn or have the desire to learn and they deal with the same negative things in their lives year after year, and I say it STOPS right now in Jesus' Name! When you first received Jesus Christ as your Lord and Savior you started a new process in life, which is salvation from eternal damnation to eternal life and it came instantly, but the process of renewing your mind takes time and effort (Romans 12:1-2). Renewing our mind is up to us, it's not God's job. The prayer of salvation is not a cure-all, what I am saying is that a prayer doesn't change your "stinking thinking" or change your bad habits that have been developed for years. When you receive Jesus on the inside there should be a desire to change, but having a desire to change doesn't mean that you will change. It's just like if you have a desire to own a Mercedes-Benz, that does not mean that you will have one. That desire must be put into action with self-discipline, and you have to put yourself in a position to buy a Mercedes-Benz. It's the same desire that we must have in Christ that has to be turned into action and obedience to His Word, and the love you have for what Christ did for you must propel you into a life with no regrets. Living a life of holiness is a must, so therefore you must go through the process of change, but most of all you must put the right things in the process like reading your Bible on a regular basis, having fellowship with strong believers, and leaving the past behind—including the people in your past that do not want to live for God and move forward in the process. You must get delivered from the opinions of people or what others think of you, because ultimately it is between you and God.

Chapter 5

OUTLOOK DETERMINE OUTCOME

The process is a way of life, and in life you will go through many processes that you cannot avoid. It is the way you go through them and what you do while you are in the process that determines how long you will stay in the process. What we do has everything to do with the outcome and the amount of time we spend in the process. A good example of this is the children of Israel as they were leaving Egypt and headed to the Promised Land. They physically left Egypt, but when challenges and difficulties came their first response was to blame Moses and God. The children of Israel were still not in Egypt, but their minds went back to slavery and bondage even though they were physically free.

So what is your Egypt? Think about when hard times hit—we revert back to the very things that held us captive. This is because staying in bondage, slavery, and sin takes no effort. It becomes easy because it is in our nature, and in order to come out of Egypt mentally we have to make the choice to renew our minds. That's why our prison system if full of men in their 40's, 50's, and 60's because they did not have it in them to start or stay in the process of change, which made it hard for them. If they had started the process of change, they couldn't stay with it simply because it was too hard on their flesh and they didn't want to change. Just like the children of Israel, they stayed in the process for 40 years and went around the same mountain over and over again because they couldn't trust God and couldn't get over their past.

So what is your mountain that you have been going around time and time again for years? God is so serious about leaving the past behind and trusting Him that He did not allow the ones that didn't or couldn't change to enter into the Promised Land. God is serious about process, so we must also take it very seriously, since the only ones who entered into the Promised Land were those who left the past behind, trusted the Lord, and made it through the process. Even Moses himself didn't get to see the Promised Land because he was more focused on the opinions of men than he was on the promises of God. Therefore, the ones that didn't change their minds in the wilderness were not able to enter into the Promised Land. Thank God we live under the dispensation of Grace now and can enter into our Promised Land that He has for us!

What is the wilderness? It's the period of time from which you left the past and headed to a great life in God. It's the holding place in the process and it's in this wilderness that you find God! If you don't find God and start obeying Him and His Word while in the process, you will never make it to the Promised Land, will die in the wilderness, and will never fulfill your purpose here on earth. So, if you are in the wilderness right now in your life and the path you are walking down is very frustrating for you, then give it up and turn towards God. The Bible says if WE draw close to God then HE will draw close to us. We have to make the first move towards God, so take this time to allow Him to show you what you need to change in your life and make the necessary adjustments to stop going around the same mountain over and over again. To start moving towards the Promised Land, trust me, it's well worth all the work. I am living a life today that 20 years ago seemed like just a dream. For over 10 years, I would start the process, then it would get hard and I would bail out. I would begin to put a lot of pain and suffering on my loved ones, but then I would snap out of the sin cycle in my life, which caused me to start the process over again. This cycle continued for many years until I finally made it up my mind that I needed to change and was willing to do whatever it took to change. I did whatever it took to get rid of the hurts from my past and my childhood because I was sick of going around the same mountain in my life. Nothing changed in my life until I changed. My business didn't start growing until I started growing. I am so glad I stayed in the process and relied on the pros of the process, which are extremely essential to the process. These basic principles will help you make it through any process in your life, as long as you properly apply them.

Chapter 6

THE ESSENTIALS TO APPLY
IN THE PROCESS

1. Accept the process You must accept where you're at in life and must understand that you didn't get into the state you're in overnight. Accepting it doesn't mean you have to stay in your mess, it simply means that you know and understand where you are, and that you are willing and ready to take full responsibility to stop blaming others for your dysfunctional thinking and behavior. Submit your life to the Lord 100% and let Him do what He needs to do in you and know that He who began a perfect work in you will complete it until the day of Jesus Christ. (Philippians 1:6).

2. See the pros in the process The Lord is at work, so look at the good things that are taking place in your life. Even though it might not be real fun at times, it is a great thing taking place. Remember, outlook determines outcome. Focus on all the positive things that are beginning to happen in your life. It is a process, after all, and it will happen for you as long as you don't give up!!

3. **Don't abort the process** If you bail out of the process temporarily and say, "I can't do this," when you go back in the process, you start completely all over again from the beginning. So the best thing to do is stay in the process and go through it. You didn't get in your mess overnight so it does take time. Just like the human gestation period of a baby, which, start to finish is a 9 month period going through lots of different processes along the way, the same applies to this. You can have a life you can only dream of and can turn it into a reality if you don't abort the process.

4. **Grow in the process** It's in the process that you find God. It's where you accept responsibility for the good and the not so good in your life. Allow God to change you, and you must also make the necessary changes. Learn from your mistakes and the mistakes of others. Be like a tree and plant yourself next to the river of living water. Allow your roots to go down and grow where God plants you, for the meantime. You must put yourself in an environment that enables growth. Don't stay home and

do nothing, still expecting to grow. It's time to get up and find a church where you can grow because the church is the avenue through which God has chosen to move on the earth.

The necessary elements in the pros of process are learn, change, and grow. These three things are essential in becoming everything God has called you to be. You must be open to learn, no matter your age. You don't know it all, so a teachable spirit is a must. Knowledge is power, and wisdom is the principle thing. So apply what you learn and you will never go through the same processes ever again. In life, you will always be in a process because it's the way of life. You can't avoid it, but the process we are talking about here is the process of coming out of sin and into a great life in God. You must be flexible and grow in allowing God to show you things about yourself and humble yourself with true humility. The Bible says God resists the proud but gives grace to the humble. (James 4:6) If you want grace in the process then humble yourself, put on true humility, and completely repent.

Chapter 7

THE PROCESS OF SANCTIFICATION

Sanctification is a process. It is the act and process of acquiring sanctity, of being made or becoming holy. In Thessalonians 4:3, the Bible states that sanctification is God's will for us. You can say that it is the state of proper functioning. When we receive Jesus Christ as our Lord and Savior, we are immediately justified. Justification happens immediately because it is a spiritual experience from God and has nothing to do with our own merit, concerning any type of work we have to do or even could do. Jesus paid the price for us to be justified, so we just have to believe and receive. Now, sanctification comes from what we do with ourselves, and the only way for the process of sanctification to take place in our lives is by renewing our mind with the Word of God. See Romans 12:2, Ephesians 5:26.

The process of moving into sanctification doesn't happen overnight—it's an ongoing process for the rest of our lives. It is a progression of moving forward in our minds, from faith to faith and glory to glory. The more sanctified you become, the farther away you move from your past and the farther from past hurts and failures. You have to spend more time with God and in His Word than you ever have spent in your life. It comes down to how bad you want a better life. To have something that you have never had, you must do something that you have never done. Focus on that statement, it is so powerful. You can't keep living the way you are living and expect a better life. Sanctification is a constant and continual process through a yielded vessel by the working of the Holy Spirit in our lives. We must do our part by reading the Bible and getting a fresh revelation of who Jesus Christ really is in our lives. He loves us very much and wants us to be all we can be for Him and to be used for His glory because He can't use broken, wounded, messed up, and hurt people. This is a process we all must go through by digging our heels into the ground and make the choice to say, "I won't be moved," open your heart to the movement of God, and stay in the process of sanctification.

Chapter 8

THE PROCESS OF PAIN

The process of pain and the process of sanctification are very similar. The hardest thing for a person to do is change. The process of change usually involves pain—pain from the past, pain from a broken heart, pain from childhood molestation, pain from childhood abuse, pain from being rejected by family or friends, and pain from anything put on you that wasn't from God.

If your life is like a roller-coaster—always up and down—or if you do good for a while but you always keep going back to the past and keep falling back into sin, it's because you avoid dealing with the issues of the heart. Talking about it or trying to overcome it is too much pain for you to handle. That's why we avoid good people who are actually trying to help us.

The old saying "no pain, no gain" is so very true in what we are talking about here in the process of pain. This is actually one of the Pros of Process. Going through it may not seem like a positive thing, but it is very positive. We must dig all the old roots out of our life in order to have a great life in God, but it is painful and this part of the process is where most people will bail out of the process because of this pain. Talking about the past and rehearsing something from the past that hurt you is very painful, I know. But when it is all over you will never hurt again from a particular situation. It's only painful because you have never faced it or faced yourself, so you haven't given yourself a chance to get healed from it. When you go through the process of pain and come out the other side, you are made whole. The old roots got pulled out of your life, the old sin that is trying to hang on is gone, and the pain is gone because you got completely healed. So stick with it and hang in there because all the pain is worth it. The Bible says that sorrow may last for a night but joy comes in the morning. (Psalms 30:5) I have gone through this process at four different times in my life about four different things that have caused pain in my life, and let me tell you, it is well worth it. I am living a life today that twenty years ago was just a dream, and it's even better than what I could have come up with on my own. I had to dig up every old root in my life, and I had help through it with a person I knew well, trusted, and that knew my situation. It is vital to find someone you trust that has the ability to help you through part of the process because forgiveness is a major factor here. You must forgive those who have hurt you.

You must let go! You must let go of every bad thing in the past that is causing you pain. Do yourself a favor and forgive those that have hurt you or disappointed you. Get rid of it and let it go. It's only holding you back from your purpose and keeping you from walking in the greatness God has for you. Before I forgave those that have wronged me and got rid of the things that I was holding on to, it was actually hurting me, not the person that hurt me. I kept going back into sin because of it. So I put myself through the process and it was painful, but if you keep on pushing through and allow the Lord to heal your heart, it won't last forever. You will have a great life ahead of you. If you are still dipping and diving and in and out of sin, it's probably because you have unhealed hurts in your life and also some unforgiveness. "No pain, no gain" is right. Once the pain is gone, you gained your whole life and your family's life as well. It's just like childbirth, which is one of the most painful things ever. The point where the baby is coming out is the point of most pain (that's what my wife told me). But once it's over, you get to look at the beautiful reward you received. If you're a man, you didn't go through the pain of birth but you get to also enjoy the great reward of it. Getting all the sin and hurts out of your life is the same way, and if you help someone through the pain of it all, you get to enjoy the reward for years to come. You can do it. Don't give up!!

Chapter 9

PROCESS OF JUSTIFICATION

The definition of justification is the act, process, or state of being justified by God. An acceptable reason for doing something or something that justifies an action. The act or an instance of proving to be just, right, or reasonable.

In the realm of being a Christian, justification isn't something we can do, it's something only God can do. It's not by our works, it's all about Him. The process of justification is the easiest process to go through, because all you have to do is accept it and receive it by faith.

Justification means to be declared not guilty of all sin and cleared of any penalties against God's law. God treats those who are justified as righteous and treats them as if they have kept all of His laws. We cannot justify ourselves by any work we do because our works cannot meet up to God's standards. Romans

2:23 states, "For all have sinned and fall short of the glory of God."

Justification is a gift from God. Romans 3:24, and we are justified by His grace as a gift.The gift of justification is Christ taking our place in judgment by paying for our sins on the cross. At the cross, we gave Christ our sin and He gave us His righteousness. 2 Corinthians 5:21 states, "For our sake He made Him to be sin who knew no sin, so that in Him we might become the righteousness of God." These are the basics of justification, and before you can go through any other process in your life, you must understand this process, accept it, and receive it by faith. So, you can relieve yourself of all the guilt and shame from the mistakes and bad choices of your past.

Chapter 10

THE PROCESS OF BECOMING

This is the part of the process where you start to see all your hard work paying off. It is where everything starts clicking and making sense while you're in the process. It's the reward for not quitting and not giving up on yourself. You start seeing yourself in a whole new way, and you see yourself how God sees you. You become everything that God has intended for you to be so you can fulfill the calling on your life. This is the goal that you are working toward. God has called you to greatness, and the process of becoming is the beauty of it all. You can make it, and this is the part of the process you want to be in. Staying in this is where you find joy, peace, love, and patience. It is where you thrive, where you will accomplish great things in your life. When you get to this process, nothing from your past can hold you back ever again. It is where you win because you didn't give up. If you don't quit, then you will win and get to this place. It will be easy to stay in this place. You are more than a conqueror—you're an overcomer, and you can do it!

SALVATION PRAYER

Dear God in heaven, I come to you in the name of Jesus. I acknowledge to You that I am a sinner, and I am sorry for my sins and the life that I have lived; I need your forgiveness.

I believe that your only begotten Son Jesus Christ shed His precious blood on the cross at Calvary and died for my sins, and I am now willing to turn from my sin.

You said in Your Holy Word, Romans 10:9 that if we confess the Lord our God and believe in our hearts that God raised Jesus from the dead, we shall be saved.

Right now, I confess Jesus as the Lord of my soul. With my heart, I believe that God raised Jesus from the dead. This very moment I accept Jesus Christ as my own personal Savior and according to His Word, right now I am saved.

Thank you, Jesus, for your unlimited grace which has saved me from my sins. I thank you Jesus that your grace never leads to license, but rather it always leads to repentance. Therefore, Lord Jesus transform my life so that I may bring glory and honor to you alone and not to myself.

Thank you, Jesus, for dying for me and giving me eternal life. AMEN.

If you prayed this prayer, we would like to know. Please let us know by emailing us or posting on our Facebook page. Bless you!

ASHTON GRANITE DESIGN, LLC.

Ashton Granite Design LLC
4720 E. Admiral PL Suite C
Tulsa OK 74116
www.ashtongranite.com
office 918-986-8550
cell 918-630-0745
email ashtongranite@yahoo.com also
prosofprocess@gmail.com

Follow us at Ashton Granite on;

Facebook
Instagram
Twitter
LinkedIn

www.ingramcontent.com/pod-product-compliance
Lightning Source LLC
Chambersburg PA
CBHW060630030426
42337CB00018B/3282